• 中国圣人文化丛书 •
CHINESE SAGES SERIES

孟子名言录

QUOTATIONS FROM MENCIUS

编注　蔡希勤
英译　何祚康
　　　郁　苓
绘图　李士伋

华语教学出版社
北　京

First Edition 2002

ISBN 7-80052-806-5

Published by Sinolingua
24 Baiwanzhuang Road, Beijing 100037, China
Tel: 86-10-68325871
86-10-68996333
Fax: 86-10-68326333
E-mail: sinolingua@ihw.com.cn
Printed by Beijing Foreign Languages Printing House
Distributed by China International
Book Trading Corporation
35 Chegongzhuang Xilu, P.O. Box 399
Beijing 100044, China

Printed in the People's Republic of China

编者的话

孟子曰:“言近而指远者，善言也。”

孟子是中国儒家学派重要代表人物，孔子后一人，被尊为“亚圣”，儒家文化亦被称为“孔孟之道”。他在修身养性、治国安民、教育学习、交友处世、孝亲敬老等方面为我们留下了很多充满智慧和哲理的警世名言，其中不少至今仍具有现实的教育意义。我们从中选取一部分言简意赅，便于记诵的话结集成这本《孟子名言录》出版，并配以英文和精美插图，供广大中外青少年读者欣赏。

Compiler's Notes

"Simple words with far-reaching meaning are good words." This is one of the profound sayings of Mencius, an outstanding exponent of the Confucian school. He was honored as the "Lesser Sage," and Confucianism is often referred to as "the teachings of Confucius and Mencius."

A precious legacy of Mencius is his remarks on many topics, such as self-cultivation, education and learning, government and the people, human relations and making friends, and fraternal duty and filial piety. Many of these celebrated dictums are still very educational and enlightening today.

We have selected from the treasure house of his sayings some short quotations which are easy to read and memorize. Accompanied by the English translation and illustrations, they promise a very enjoyable and rewarding experience for Chinese and foreign readers alike.

目　录

Contents

为 学 篇

On Learning

人之患在好为人师。

《孟子·离娄上》

The trouble with people is that they are too eager to assume the role of teacher.

患：(huàn)，忧虑，担心。**好为人师：**好（hào)，喜欢，不谦虚，喜欢以教导者自居。

孟子说：“人最怕总喜欢做人家的老师。”

人之所不学而能者，其良能也；所不虑而知者，其良知也。

《孟子·尽心上》

What men can do without learning is a result of inborn ability; what men know without contemplating is a result of intuition.

良能：天赋最好的能力。不用学习而自然就能者，是谓良能也。也就是孔子说的“生而知之者”（《论语·季氏》）。**良知**：天赋的分辨是非善恶的智能。不待思虑而自然知者，是谓良知也。

孟子说：“人不待学习便能做到的，这是本能；不待思考便知道的，这是先知。”

无恒产而有恒心者，惟士为能。

《孟子·梁惠王上》

Only scholars can be morally confident though they possess no property.

孟子认为一般老百姓如果没有恒产，就不会有坚定的道德观念。就会胡作非为，违法乱纪，什么事都干得出来。所以孟子要求执政者要使老百姓的产业收入上可以赡养父母，下足以抚养妻子儿女。好年成可以丰衣足食，坏年成也不至于饿死。

孟子说：“没有恒产，而却有坚定的道德观念，只有读书人才能做到。”

博学而详说之，将以反说约也。

《孟子·离娄下》

Learn extensively, expound in detail and explain the cardinal principles briefly on the basis of mastery of knowledge.

反：回到，反回来。**约**：简略，简约。孟子这里说的是做学问由简到繁，再由繁到简的过程。

孟子说："广博地学习，详细地解说，在融会贯通的基础上再简略地述说大义。"

君子深造之以道，欲其自得之也。自得之，则居之安；居之安，则资之深；资之深，则取之左右逢其原，故君子欲其自得之也。

《孟子·离娄下》

A gentleman should advance his study in correct ways so as to acquire knowledge by himself. Once he does so, he is able to master it firmly. Firm mastery of knowledge leads to a rich accumulation of knowledge, and the use of it will be inexhaustible. So a gentleman goes all out to acquire knowledge by himself.

深造：造，诣也，进而不已之意。谓达到精深的境界。也指进一步学习和研究。**道：**正确的方法。**自得：**自己有所体会。**资：**积蓄。**取之左右逢其原：**逢，遇到；原，同"源"。成语"左右逢源"源于此。原意是做学问功夫到家，则取之不竭，用之不尽。后多指做事得心应手，顺利无阻。

孟子说："君子深造必以正确的方法，使自己有所体会。自有所得，就能牢固掌握。牢固掌握，就能积蓄深厚。积蓄深厚，便能取之不尽，左右逢源，所以君子要强调自己有所体会。"

有为者辟若掘井，掘井九轫而不及泉，犹为弃井也。

《孟子·尽心上》

Trying to achieve something is like digging a well—even if it is dug down 60 or 70 (Chinese) feet but fails to reach the spring, it is no better than an abandoned well.

轫：同“仞”，古代七尺（一说八尺）为一仞。

孟子说：“做事就像挖井一样，尽管挖了六七丈深，不见泉水仍然是一口废井。”

道在迩而求诸远，事在易而求诸难。

《孟子·离娄上》

One walks from the near to the distant and starts with the easy and moves on to the difficult.

迩：(ěr)，近。遐迩驰名（远近闻名）。

孟子说："走路由近及远，做事由易及难。"

今夫弈之为数，小数也；不专心致志，则不得也。

《孟子·告子上》

Though chess-playing is a petty skill, if one cannot devote his heart to it, he will not be able to master the skill.

弈：围棋。**数**：技巧。孟子还讲了这样一个故事："奕秋是全国的棋圣。假如让他同时教两个人，一个人专心致志，认真领会老师的讲解。另一个人虽也在听讲，而脑子里却在想入非非，心不在焉。这样，虽然他和人家一道学习，成绩肯定不如人家。这是因为他不如人家聪明吗？显然不是的。"

孟子说："譬如下围棋，这虽不过是小技艺而已，如果不能专心致志，也是学不好的。"

虽有天下易生之物也，一日暴之，十日寒之，未有能生者也。

《孟子·告子上》

Even a plant that grows readily will not be able to grow if it is exposed to the sun for one day and to the bitter cold for ten days.

一日暴之，十日寒之：暴同“曝”，晒。成语“一暴十寒”源于此。

孟子说：“就是一种最易成活的植物，如果对它晒一天，冷十天，它也是长不好的。”

予未得为孔子徒也，予私淑诸人也。

《孟子·离娄上》

I was born too late to be a disciple of Confucius; I learned from other virtuous men.

私淑：淑，善也。后遂称未得身受其教而宗仰其人为私淑。据传孟子曾“受业子思之门人”（《史记·孟荀列传》）。

孟子说：“我没能够做孔子的门徒，我是自己向诸贤人学习来的。”

孔子登东山而小鲁，登泰山而小天下，故观于海者难为水，游于圣人之门者难为言。

《孟子·尽心上》

When Confucius ascended the Eastern Mountain, he realized how small the State of Lu was. When he ascended Mount Tai, he saw how small the empire was. Anyone who has seen the sea will not be impressed by other waters. Anyone who has learned from a sage will not be attracted by other doctrines.

东山：一说即蒙山，在今山东省蒙阴县南。

孟子说："孔子登上东山往下看，便觉得鲁国小了。登上泰山，便觉得天下也小了。所以对见过大海的人，别的水就难于吸引他了；对于曾在圣人之门学习过的人，别的学说也就难于吸引他了。"

观水有术，必观其澜。

《孟子·尽心上》

There is a way to watch water, that is, to watch its roaring waves.

孟子说:“看水有个方法，一定要看它壮阔的波涛。”

学问之道无他，求其放心而已矣。

《孟子·告子上》

Learning is nothing but seeking the lost heart.

放心：放纵的心，丢失的心。孟子说："仁是人的心，义是人的路。放弃正路而不走，丧失了善良之心不知寻找，可悲呀！家里的鸡或狗丢了还知道去找，而心丢了却反而不知道去找。"所以，孟子说了上面的话。

孟子说："学问之道没有别的，就是把丧失的良心找回来罢了。"

天之高也，星辰之远也，苟求其故，千岁之日至，可坐而致也。

《孟子·离娄上》

Though the sky is extremely lofty and the stars extremely far away, if only one knew how they come to be what they are one could calculate the solar terms of one thousand years hence.

日至：此处的日至当指“冬至”。周历冬至日为“元日”。孟子和孔子一样，用启发式教授弟子，让弟子懂得举一反三和推知的道理。

孟子说：“天高星远，只要能推知其所以然，一千年后的节日也能推算出来。”

离娄之明、公输子之巧，不以规矩，不能成方圆；师旷之聪，不以六律，不能正五音。

《孟子·离娄上》

Even with Li Lou's eyesight and Gongshu Zi's skill, no one can draw a square and a circle without proper tools. Even with Shi Kuang's hearing, no one can check the five notes without the help of the six musical scales.

离娄：相传为黄帝时人，目力极强，能于百步之外看清秋毫之末。**公输子：**名般（一作“班”）鲁国人，又称鲁班。为中国古代著名巧匠。**师旷：**中国古代有名的音乐家，晋平公时任太师（乐官之长）。**六律：**指阳律六。**五音：**中国音阶名，即宫、商、角、徵、羽。

孟子说：“即使有离娄的视力，公输般的技巧，如果不借助于必要的工具，也不能画出标准的方形和圆形。即便有师旷那样的审音听力，如果不借助于六律，也不能正确校正五音。”

尽信书，则不如无书。

《孟子·尽心下》

To believe unconditionally what the *Book of History* says is worse than if there were no *Book of History* in existence.

尽信书：孟子所说的“书”指《尚书》，《武成》是书中一篇。在此篇中讲到周武王伐纣时有“血流漂杵”的记载，孟子很怀疑这记载的真实性。他认为以至仁伐至不仁，是不可能流那么多血的。

孟子说：“完全相信书，则不如没有书。”

不耻不若人，何若人有？

《孟子·尽心上》

If one does not feel ashamed to fall behind others, how can he ever catch up with them?

耻：羞耻。是孔子伦理思想的概念之一。指一种道德的羞耻感。孔子提出“行己有耻”（《论语·子路》），作为士的行为准则。他说“知耻近乎勇”（《礼记·中庸》），孟子认为羞耻心对于人关系重大。他说：“人不可以不知耻，无耻之耻无耻矣。”（《孟子·尽心上》）这种思想成为注重民族大义的知识分子的传统精神。

孟子说：“不以落后为耻，怎么能赶上别人呢？”

修身篇

On Self－Cultivation

士穷不失义，达不离道。

《孟子·尽心上》

Scholars will not drop righteousness in adversity, nor will they diverge from their principles in times of success.

穷：困厄，穷困。**达**：显贵。**道**：引申为政治路线。《论语·学而》："礼之用，和为贵，先王之道，斯为美，小大由之。"

孟子说："读书人困厄时不失义，显贵时不离道。"

古之君子过则改之；今之君子，过则顺之。

《孟子·公孙丑下》

A benevolent ruler in ancient times would correct his mistakes. But a ruler now would leave the mistake uncorrected and muddle through.

君子：在儒家学说中，君子有多种含义，此指“在位者”。**顺：**顺着。

孟子说：“古代有仁德的执政者，有错即改；今天的执政者，有了过错，竟将错就错。”

周于利者凶年不能杀，周于德者邪世不能乱。

《孟子·尽心下》

A wealthy man will not be poverty-stricken in famine years; a virtuous man will not be led astray during turbulent days.

周：足。**杀**：缺乏，有窘困意。**邪世**：乱世。

孟子说："财货富足的人荒年不受窘困，道德高尚的人乱世不会迷乱。"

养心莫善於寡欲。其为人也寡欲，虽有不存焉者，寡矣；其为人也多欲，虽有存焉者，寡矣。

《孟子·尽心下》

The best way to cultivate one's heart is to reduce one's desires. When one's desires are few, the merits that he loses will be few also. With numerous desires, one can hardly keep much goodness.

养心：修养心性。**寡欲**：少欲，节制私欲。不存、有存：指“善性”的丧失或保留。参见《孟子·离娄下》：“人之所以异于禽兽者几希，庶民去之，君子存之。”《孟子·告子上》：“虽存乎人者，岂无仁义之心哉？”

孟子说：“修养心性的方法最好是节制私欲。一个人少私欲，善性丧失就少；私欲多，其善性就不多了。”

人皆有不忍人之心。先王有不忍人之心，斯有不忍人之政矣。以不忍人之心，行不忍人之政，治天下可运之掌上。

《孟子·公孙丑上》

Everyone has a heart of mercy. Ancient kings were merciful so their governments were merciful. To practice forbearance with such a heart, running a state will be as easy as turning over one's hand.

不忍人之心：怜悯别人之心。**先王**：先秦儒家对古代圣明君主的一种称呼。

孟子说："每个人都有怜悯别人之心。先王因为有怜悯别人之心，则有怜悯别人的政治。以怜悯别人之心实施怜悯别人的政治，治理天下则易如反掌。"

恻隐之心，仁之端也；羞恶之心，义之端也；辞让之心，礼之端也；是非之心，智之端也。人之有是四端也，犹其有四体也。

《孟子·公孙丑上》

A sense of sympathy is the beginning of being benevolent; a sense of shame is the beginning of being just; a sense of modesty is the beginning of being polite; and a sense of right and wrong is the beginning of being wise. Men are born with these four senses, as with their four limbs.

端：开头。四体：四肢。

孟子说："同情心是仁的萌芽，羞耻心是义的萌芽，谦让之心是礼的萌芽，是非之心是智的萌芽。人有这四种心和有四肢一样是与生俱来的。"

仁者如射：射者正己而后发；发而不中，不怨胜己者，反求诸己而已矣。

《孟子·公孙丑上》

A benevolent man should be like an archer who takes part in a shooting match and adjusts his posture before shooting. If he misses the target, he should not blame the winners, but seek the cause in himself.

射：射箭的知识技能，古代教育内容的六艺之一。西周时，天子即以试射的办法来选拔人才。以射中次数的多少作为录用的标准。射者的行动是否合于礼仪也是评定的标准。**反求诸己：**儒家一种重要的修养方法，通过反省检验自己的思想和行为是否符合道德标准。孔子说："射有似乎君子。失诸正鹄，反求诸其身。"（《礼记·中庸》）

孟子说："有仁德的人好比参加射箭比赛的射手一样：先端正自己的姿势而后放箭，如果没有射中，也不要埋怨那些胜过自己的人，只在自己身上找原因就是了。"

今有无名之指屈而不信，非疾痛害事也，如有能信之者，则不远秦楚之路，为指之不若人也。指不若人，则知恶之；心不若人，则不知恶，此之谓不知类也。

《孟子·告子上》

A man, one of whose fingers is bent and cannot be straightened, would go all the way from Qin to Chu to have his finger cured if he knew that there were someone able to straighten it, though the bent finger hurt him not, nor did it hamper his business. It would be simply because one of his fingers was not as good as others'. He hates it when his finger is not as good as others', but he knows not how to resent it when his heart is not as good as others'. This is called ignorance of the relative importance of things.

信：同“伸”。**秦楚之路**：秦在西方，楚在南方，居中原地区的诸国以秦楚为远，形容路途遥远。**若**：像，似，如。**不知类**：朱熹《孟子集注》：“不知类，言不知轻重之等也。”

孟子说：“现在有人一个手指伸不直，虽然不痛苦，也不妨碍工作，却到处求治，如果听说有人能使它伸直，就是秦国、楚国也不以路远，一定去医治，就因为自己的一个手指头不如别人。一个手指不如别人，就知道厌恶，心性（仁）不及别人，却不知道厌恶，这叫做不知道轻重。”

口之于味也，目之于色也，耳之于声也，鼻之于臭也，四肢之于安佚也，性也，有命焉，君子不谓性也。

《孟子·尽心下》

It is human nature for the mouth to desire delicious tastes, the eyes, beautiful colors, the ears, music, the nose, fragrant smells, and the four limbs, ease. But it is fate which decides whether one can obtain these. So gentlemen do not take these as their nature.

臭：(xiù)，"臭"的本义是"气味"，不论香臭都叫"臭"，此专指芬香气味。**命**：命运。

孟子说："口对于美味，眼对于美色，耳对于好听的音乐，鼻对于香的气味，四肢对于舒服，这些爱好，都是天性，但是否能得到，却属于命运。所以君子不把这些认为是天性的必然，因此不去强求。"

人不可以无耻，无耻之耻，无耻矣。

《孟子·尽心上》

Men should not be without a sense of shame. Not knowing shame is indeed shameless.

无耻：儒家强调知耻。《礼记·中庸》："知耻近乎勇。"孔子和孟子都重视教育学生知耻。孔子说"行己以耻"（《论语·子路》）。

孟子说："人不可以没有羞耻之心，不知羞耻的那种羞耻，是真的不知羞耻。"

形色，天性也；惟圣人然后可以践形。

《孟子·尽心上》

Bodily form and appearance are endowed by Heaven. Outer beauty must be enriched by inner beauty, but this can only be done by a sage.

形色：外貌与容色。**践形**：体现人所天赋的品质。

孟子说："人的身体容貌是天生的，这种外在的美要靠内在的美来充实它，只有圣人才能做到这一点。"

爱人不亲，反其仁；治人不治，反其智；礼人不答，反其敬——行有不得者皆反求诸己，其身正而天下归之。

《孟子·离娄上》

When one loves but fails to receive love in return, one should reflect on whether one is really a benevolent man. When one fails to subject others to discipline, one should reflect on whether one knows the proper way to govern. When one fails to gain respect from others while treating others with the proper courtesies, one should reflect on whether one is sincere enough. One should reflect on oneself whenever one fails to get the expected results. If a ruler behaves correctly, all the people will pay allegiance to him.

反其仁、反其智、反其敬： 反问自身的意思。**反求诸己：** 参见孔子的“反求诸其身”（《礼记·中庸》）。

孟子说：“爱别人，却得不到别人的爱，就要反问自己是否真正有仁爱之心。管理别人，却没有管理好，就要反省自己的管理方法是否正确，知识是否够用。以礼待人却得不到别人的尊重，就要反责自己对别人的态度是否真诚。任何行为如果没有得到预期的效果都要反躬自责，自己的确端正了，天下人便会归向他。”

人皆有所不忍，达之于其所忍，仁也；人皆有所不为，达之于其所为，义也。

《孟子·尽心上》

Everyone has something that he cannot bear. To extend such aversion to what he can bear is benevolence. Everyone has something that he refuses to do. To extend such aversion to what he is willing to do is righteousness.

不忍：不忍心干的事。**达**：扩充，扩大。**不为**：不忍为。

孟子说："每个人都有不忍心干的事，把这种心情扩充到所忍心干的事上，便是仁。每个人都有不肯干的事，把它扩充到所肯干的事上，便是义。"

反身而诚，乐莫大焉。强恕而行，求仁莫近焉。

《孟子·尽心上》

There can be no greater pleasure than to find, after reflection, oneself sincere. Persisting in treating others in the way one wishes to be treated is the shortest way to benevolence.

反身：儒家一种修养方法，指通过反省来检验自己的思想和行为是否符合道德标准，即“反求诸其身”（《礼记·中庸》）。**恕**：孔子的伦理范畴之一，有推己及人，即希望别人以对己的态度来对待别人之意。孔子说：“其恕乎，己所不欲，勿施于人。”（《论语·卫灵公》）**近**：近路，捷径。

孟子说：“反躬自问，自己是真诚的，便是最大的快乐。坚持推己及人的恕道，这是达到仁德的捷径。”

五谷者，种之美者也；苟为不熟，不如荑稗。

《孟子·告子上》

The five kinds of grain are the best species of crops. But they are no more useful than weeds if they are not properly ripe.

荑稗：两种草名。荑即稊（tì），和稗（bài）一样，都是杂草，结实甚小，但可作家畜饲料，古人也用以备凶年。孟子这里以五谷喻仁。

孟子说："五谷虽然是庄稼中的好品种，假若不能成熟，反而不及稊稗有用。"

耻之于人大矣，为机变之巧者，无所用耻焉。

《孟子·尽心上》

A sense of shame is of great importance to men. Cunning and crafty men have no sense of shame.

机变：机械的巧变。

孟子说："羞耻对于人关系重大，机谋巧诈之人是不知道羞耻的。"

穷则独善其身，达则兼善天下。

《孟子·尽心上》

In obscurity, scholars would maintain their own integrity. In times of success, they would make perfect the whole empire.

独善、兼善：独善，保持个人的节操。兼善，不仅求得自身的善，并且使别人也达到善的境界。

孟子说："穷困时则独善其身，显贵时则兼善天下。"

独孤臣孽子，其操心也危，其虑患也深，故达。

《孟子·尽心上》

Only estranged ministers and sons born by concubines know all, because they are in a state of constant caution and great worry.

孽子：古代一夫多妻，非嫡妻所生之子叫庶子，也叫孽子，地位卑贱。**危**：不安，谨慎。**达**：通达事理。

孟子说："只有那些孤臣孽子，他们由于谨言慎行，忧虑深刻，所以能通达事理。"

令闻广誉施于身，所以不愿人之文绣也。

《孟子·告子上》

When one enjoys a good reputation in society, one does not hanker after others' finery.

令闻：好名声。**文绣：**古代必须有爵命的人才能着文绣之服。

孟子说："自己身上有社会公认的美名，也就不会羡慕别人的锦衣绣服了。"

欲贵者，人之同心也。人人有贵于己者，弗思耳矣。人之所贵者，非良贵也。

《孟子·告子上》

Everyone shares the aspiration for honor. Everyone has something honorable in himself he has never noticed. Honor bestowed by others is not true honor.

弗：不，弗思，不去想。**良贵：**真正的尊贵。

孟子说："希望尊贵，这是人们共有的心理。但每个人自身都有可尊贵的东西，只是不肯认真想它罢了。别人所给的尊贵，不是真正的尊贵。"

天下之言性也，则故而已矣。故者以利为本。

《孟子·离娄上》

When one talks about the nature of something, he needs to know how it comes to be what it is, and the key to knowing this is to see how it functions.

性：本性。**利**：顺。

孟子说：“天下人论本性，只要能知道其所以然就行了。推求其所以然的基础是顺其自然之理。”

人病舍其田而芸人之田——所求于人者重，而所以自任者轻。

《孟子·尽心下》

The trouble with some lies in neglecting their own fields but cultivating the fields of others—they are strict with others, but lenient with themselves.

舍其田而芸人之田：孟子的意思是舍弃自身操守的修养而去帮助别人去修养自身。**芸：**除草，通“耘”。

孟子说：“有些人的毛病在于放弃自己的田地，却去到别人田里除草——要求别人严，对待自己宽。”

富贵不能淫，贫贱不能移，
威武不能屈，此之谓大丈夫。

《孟子·滕文公下》

Wealth and power cannot corrupt him, poverty can not sway his principles and threats cannot made him bend. Only such a person can be called a gentleman.

孟子说:“富贵不能乱其心，贫贱不能变其志，威武不能屈其节，这才是大丈夫。”

君子之志于道也，不成章不达。

《孟子·尽心上》

Gentlemen, in their pursuit of principles, will not reach enlightenment without making some achievements first.

成章：一定的成就。

孟子说：“君子有志于道，不取得一定的成就，也就不能通达。”

我善养吾浩然之气。

《孟子·公孙丑上》

I am good at cultivating the great moral force.

浩然之气： 正大刚直之气。也省称浩然。那么什么叫浩然之气呢？孟子说："这很难一下子讲清楚。这种气至大至刚。用正义去培养它，不能稍有伤害，这种气就会存在于天地之间，无所不在。这种气还必须和义与道相配合，否则就没有什么力量了。这种气是由正义的长期积累所产生的，不是一朝一夕所能取得的。只要做一件于心有愧的事，这种气就空了。"

孟子说："我善于培养我的浩然之气。"

故天将降大任于是人也，必先苦其心志，劳其筋骨，饿其体肤，空乏其身，行拂乱其所为，所以动心忍性，曾益其所不能。

《孟子·告子下》

When Heaven intends to bestow a great mission on a person, it makes him suffer in mind and body. It makes him endure starvation, and subjects him to poverty, difficulties and all kinds of tests so as to harden his will power, toughen his nature and increase his capabilities.

心志：心意，志向。**忍性**：坚忍其性。**曾**：同“增”。**所不能**：原来没有的，不会的知识（技能）。

孟子说：“天将要把重大使命赋予某人时，必先苦其心志，劳其筋骨，饿其体肤，使他穷困让他历经磨炼，这样，便可以坚强他的心，坚韧他的性情，增长他的能力。”

天下有道，以道殉身；天下无道，以身殉道。

《孟子·尽心上》

When the rule of the empire is in order, a gentleman immerses himself in principles. When the rule of the state is in disorder, a gentleman will not spare his own life to practice principles.

以道殉身：“道”为“身”（己）所运用。意为天下政治清明，“道”因之得以施行。**以身殉道：**“身”（己）为“道”而牺牲。意为天下政治黑暗，君子不惜为道不能施行而献身。

孟子说：“天下政治清明，道因之得以施行；天下政治黑暗，君子不惜为道不能施行而献身。”

处世篇

On Human Relations

言人之不善，当如后患何。

《孟子·离娄下》

What shall a man do when he meets with some misfortune in the future if he talks about others' shortcomings now?

言人之不善：儒家主张责己严，待人宽。孔子主张“君子成人之美，不成人之恶”（《论语·颜渊》）。《大戴礼·曾子立事》：“君子已善，亦乐人之善也。己能，亦乐人之能也。”

孟子说：“尽说别人的坏话，日后祸患来了，自己怎么办呢？”

人有不为也，而后可以有为。

《孟子·离娄下》

A person can make some achievement only when there is something that he does not do.

不为、有为：不作为；有所作为。

孟子说："人要有所不为，才能有所为。"

西子蒙不洁，则人皆掩鼻而过之；虽有恶人，齐戒沐浴，则可以祀上帝。

《孟子·离娄下》

If Xi Zi were covered in filth, everyone would pass her by holding his nose. If an ugly man fasts and bathes he may offer sacrifices to the Lord of Heaven.

西子：古代美女西施。**恶人**：面貌丑陋的人。**齐**：同“斋”。

孟子说：“如果西施满身肮脏，别人也会掩鼻而过；纵是面貌丑陋的人，如果斋戒沐浴，也可以祭祀上帝。”

无为其所不为，无欲其所不欲，如此而已矣。

《孟子·尽心上》

Do not do what you should not do, and do not desire what you should not desire. That is all.

无为：儒家指以德政感化人民，不施行刑治。《论语·卫灵公》：“无为而治者，其舜也与。夫何为哉，恭己正南面而已矣。”**欲：**私欲，贪欲。

孟子说：“不干不应干的事，不要不应要的东西，这样就行了。”

挟太山以超北海，语人曰，“我不能。”是诚不能也。为长者折枝，语人曰，“我不能。”是不为也，非不能也。

《孟子·梁惠王上》

One really means it when he tells another: "I cannot hold Mount Tai under my arms and carry it across the North Sea." But when he tells another: "I am unable to break a branch from a tree for an old man," what he really means is he will not do it, not that he is unable to do it.

太山：泰山。**北海**：渤海。**折枝**：有三种解释：① 折取树枝。② 弯腰行礼。③ 按摩搔痒。

孟子对齐宣王说："如果对人说挟起泰山跨越北海的事我做不到，这是真的做不到。但如果对人说为老人折取树枝的事我做不到，这是不肯去做，而不是做不到。"

恭者不侮人，俭者不夺人。

《孟子·离娄上》

A courteous man will not insult others; a self-restrained man will not rob others.

侮：(wǔ) 欺负，凌辱。**夺**：(duó) 强取。

孟子说："有礼貌的人不会侮辱别人，节俭的人不会掠夺别人。"

权，然后知轻重；度，然后知长短。物皆然，心为甚。

《孟子·梁惠王上》

One knows the weight after weighing it and one knows the distance after measuring it. This principle applies to all things, and especially to popular feelings.

权：称锤，测定物体重量的器具，亦指称重量。**度**：计量长短的标准。

孟子对齐宣王说："称一称，才知道轻重；量一量，才知道长短。什么东西都是这样，人心更是如此。"

君子莫大乎与人为善。

《孟子·公孙丑上》

The best virtue of a gentleman is to do good things for the benefit of others.

与人为善：助人相与为善。

孟子说："君子最高的德行就是与人为善。"

伯夷隘，柳下惠不恭。隘与不恭，君子不由也。

《孟子·公孙丑上》

Boyi was narrow-minded and Liuxia Hui was not serious enough. No gentleman should be like that.

伯夷：商末孤竹君长子。初孤竹君以次子叔齐为继承人，后兄弟二人为推让君位而共同出走，投奔周。但又反对周武王进军讨伐商王朝。武王灭商后，他们逃避到首阳山，不食周粟而饿死。被儒家尊为“古之贤人”。孔子对其很是赞赏，孟子对他却有微辞。**隘**（ài），狭窄。**柳下惠**：春秋时鲁国大夫。展氏，名获，字禽。食邑柳下，私谥惠，故又称柳下惠。以善于讲究贵族礼仪著称。孔子赞为“贤者”，孟子却说他太随便。**由**：经历，为。

孟子说：“伯夷器量太小；柳下惠太随便。器量小和太随便都是君子所不为的。”

规矩，方员之至也；圣人，人伦之至也。

《孟子·离娄上》

The compass and the T-square are the criteria of circles and squares. Sages are the criterion of human relationships.

规矩：校正圆形、方形的器具。**员**：同“圆”。**至**：极。**人伦**：阶级社会里人的等级关系。“使契为司徒，教以人伦；父子有亲，君臣有义，夫妇有别，长幼有叙，朋友有信”（《孟子·滕文公上》）。

孟子说：“规矩是方圆的准则，圣人是做人的准则。”

顺天者存，逆天者亡。

《孟子·离娄上》

Those who follow Heaven's will survive and those who disobey Heaven's will perish.

孟子认为："国家政治清明，道德低的人听命于道德高的人，一般人听命于贤人。国家政治黑暗，力量大的奴役力量小的，强的奴役弱的。这两种情况都是由天命决定的。"

孟子说："天命是不可违的。顺从天命者生存，违背天命者灭亡。"

可以取，可以无取，取伤廉；
可以与，可以无与，与伤惠；
可以死，可以无死，死伤勇。

《孟子·离娄下》

It would be corruption to take if one could choose between "to take" and "not to take". It would not be a favor to give if one could choose between "to give" and "not to give". It would not be courage to die if one could choose between "to die" and "not to die".

伤惠、伤勇：过去一般人认为："可以与，可以无与，则宜与；可以死，可以无死，则宜死。"孟子却反其道，提出"与伤惠，死伤勇"。意思是恩惠不是指小恩小惠，勇敢不是轻生。毛奇龄《圣门释非录》引元儒金履祥之言曰："此必战国之世，豪侠之习胜，多轻施结客，若四豪之类；刺客轻生，若荆聂之类，故孟子为当时戒耳。"

孟子说："可取可不取，取则有损廉洁。可给可不给，给则有损恩惠。可死可不死，死则有损勇敢。"

非礼之礼，非义之义，大人弗为。

《孟子·离娄下》

A man of virtue will not observe specious rites, nor will he administer specious justice.

非：诋毁，讥讽。大人：德高之人。

孟子说："似是而非的礼，似是而非的义，道德高尚的人是不干的。"

仰不愧于天，俯不怍于人。

《孟子·尽心上》

The second delight of a gentleman is that he feels no shame as he faces Heaven above and the people here below.

怍：惭愧。

孟子说："上无愧于天，下无愧于人，是人生最快乐的事。"

如知其非义，斯速已矣，何待来年？

《孟子·滕文公下》

If one recognizes that his behavior is wrong, he should correct it as soon as possible. Why wait until next year?

何待来年：宋国大夫戴盈之说：“税率十分抽一，免除关卡和商品税，现在一下子办不到，准备先减轻一些，等到明年再完全实行，你看怎么样？”孟子说：“现在有一个人每天偷邻居家一只鸡，有人告诉他说：‘这不是君子行为。’他便说：‘我一下子改不掉这毛病，先改为每月偷一只鸡，等到明年再完全不偷。’”

孟子说“如果知道这行为是错误的，便应尽快改正，为什么要等到以后再改正呢。”

非其道，则一箪食不可受于人；如其道，则舜受尧之天下，不以为泰。

《孟子·滕文公下》

I would not accept even one meal if it was not taken in accordancne with the right way. It was not excessive for Shun to take over the empire from Yao because it was taken according to the right way.

箪：（dān），盛饭的竹器。**舜受尧之天下：**尧和舜，传为上古帝王。舜名重华，号有虞氏，史称虞舜。生于妫汭（今山西永济），年二十以孝闻名。在尧晚年因四岳举荐，代尧摄政。尧死后登帝位。**泰：**过甚。

孟子说："如果不合理，连一顿饭也不可以接受。如果合理，像舜接受了尧的天下，也不以为过。"

志士不忘在沟壑，勇士不忘丧其元。

《孟子·滕文公下》

A person with lofty ideals would not hesitate to have his corpse abandoned in the wilderness, and a courageous person would not spare his life to do what is right.

志士：有远大志向的人。**沟壑**：山沟，坑。**丧**：失去。**元**：头，首。

孟子说："有志之士为坚守节操不怕弃尸荒野，勇敢的人见义而为不怕掉脑袋。"

得志，与民由之；不得志，独行其道。

《孟子·滕文公下》

When a gentleman is in power, he should follow the right course together with the people; when he is not in power, he should still stick to his principles.

由：走，经历。

孟子说："得志时，和百姓一起走正道；不得志的时候，也能独自坚持正确的原则。"

为高必因丘陵，为下必因川泽；为政不因先王之道，可谓智乎？

《孟子·离娄上》

Lofty platforms should be built on mountains; deep ponds should be dug in marshes. Would it be wise to run a state without following the ways of the ancient sages?

因：依靠，根据。**先王之道**：圣王之道。儒家特指古代圣王尧、舜、禹，文、武、周公及商汤的治国之道，其根本内容是礼乐制度和仁义道德。

孟子说："筑高台要凭借山陵，挖深池要凑沼泽之地。如果治理国家不凭借前代圣王之道，那能说是聪明吗？"

为政篇

On Government

不信仁贤，则国空虚；无礼义，则上下乱；无政事，则财用不足。

《孟子·尽心下》

If virtuous and talented men are not trusted, then the state will be devoid of all good men. If the rites are not observed, then the relations between superior and inferior will be in confusion. If a government is not properly administered, then the state's resources will fail.

空虚：没有人才。孟子的意思是如果执政者不能重视人才，那么有才能的人就会流失。**上下：**上下级官吏。**政事：**政治。

孟子说："不信任仁德贤能的人，国家就会无人才选用；没有礼仪，上下级的关系就会混乱；没有好的政治，国家财政就会困难。"

以佚道使民，虽劳不怨。以生道杀民，虽死不怨杀者。

《孟子·尽心上》

If people are employed in order to ease their lot, they will not begrudge it even if they are driven hard. If people are killed for the sake of saving others' lives, even those who are killed will not begrudge those who kill them.

佚：安乐，通“逸”。**生**：活着，生活着。

孟子说：“为了老百姓的安乐而役使百姓，百姓虽劳苦而无怨。为了老百姓的生命安全而杀死坏人，被杀者也不会怨恨杀他的人。”

上有好者，下必有甚焉者矣。君子之德，风也；小人之德，草也。草尚之风，必偃。

《孟子·滕文公上》

Inferiors are keen to do more of what their superiors are fond of doing. Gentlemen are like the wind and petty persons are like grass, which bends with the wind.

尚：同上。古“上”与“尚”常通用。**偃**：(yǎn)，卧倒，倒伏。

孟子说：“在上位的人有什么爱好，下边的人一定爱得更加过分。君子好比风，小人好比草，风向哪边吹，草向哪边倒。”

小固不可以敌大，寡固不可以敌众，弱固不可以敌强。

《孟子·梁惠王上》

It seems that a small kingdom cannot defeat a big kingdom, a sparsely populated kingdom cannot defeat a densely populated kingdom, nor can a weak kingdom defeat a powerful kingdom.

小固不可以敌大：这是孟子对齐宣王说的话，当时齐宣王欲效“齐桓、晋文”之事，孟子则劝他行仁政而统一天下，否则靠齐国的武力要征服天下的想法不过是“缘木求鱼”而已。

孟子说：“小国不可能征服大国，人口稀少的国家不可能征服人口众多的国家，弱国不可能征服强国。”

古之人未尝不欲仕也，又恶不由其道。不由其道而往者，与钻穴隙之类也。

《孟子·滕文公下》

Of our forefathers none eschewed officialdom. But they hated to become officials without going through the proper procedure. To be an official without going through the proper procedure is like becoming engaged to be married privately: Everyone would look down upon such an official.

钻穴隙之类也：孟子曰："丈夫生而愿为之有室，女子生而愿为之有家；父母之心，人皆有之。不待父母之命，媒妁之言，钻穴隙相窥，逾墙相从，则父母国人皆贱之。"（《孟子·滕文公下》）

孟子说："古人不是不想做官，而是讨厌不经正当途径而获得官位。不经正当途径而做官，正像男女私定终身一样为人瞧不起。"

言无实不祥。不祥之实，蔽贤者当之。

《孟子·离娄下》

It is not right to utter empty words; empty words come from those who stifle criticism and suggestions.

实：与“虚”相对。可理解为结果，内容。**祥**：好，吉利。**蔽**：遮挡。

孟子说：“言之无物是不好的，这是由堵塞贤路者造成的。”

诸侯之宝三：土地，人民，政事。宝珠玉者，殃必及身。

《孟子·尽心下》

For the lords of the states there are three treasures: land, people and government. Those who value pearls and jade above these are sure to bring disaster on themselves.

孟子说："诸侯有三宝：土地，百姓和政治。如果以珍珠美玉为宝，一定会祸及其身。"

以力服人者，非心服也，力不赡也；以德服人者，中心悦而诚服也。如七十子之服孔子也。

《孟子·公孙丑上》

When one dominates others by force, they do not submit to him sincerely, but do so because they are not powerful enough to resist. When one dominates others by morality, they submit gladly, as his 70 disciples respected Confucius.

赡：(shàn)，充足，丰富。“力不赡”即力不足也。**七十子：**孔子弟子中身通六艺者的通称。

孟子说：“以力服人者，人不会心服，只是因为人家没有对抗的实力；以道德服人者，人才会心悦诚服，好像孔子的七十多位弟子归服他那样。”

与谗谄面谀之人居，国欲治，可得乎？

《孟子·告子下》

Could any man administer a state well with flatterers around him all day long?

谗谄面谀之人：揣度别人心意而说些逢迎之言的人。

孟子说："整天同阿谀奉承的人在一起，能把国家治理好吗？"

入则无法家拂士，出则无敌国外患者，国恒亡。然后知生于忧患而死于安乐也。

《孟子·告子下》

A state has no chance of surviving if there are no strict, law-enforcing ministers and scholars capable of offering good advice in court and no constant threats of foreign aggression to guard against. And so we can conclude from this that worry and trouble enable one to survive, while complacency and pleasure will bring about one's downfall.

入：指国内。**法家：**指守法度的世臣。**拂士：**拂（音bì），矫正，通“弼”。指能够直谏矫正君王过失的人。**出：**指国外。

孟子说：“一个国家，国内没有执法严厉的大臣和足以辅弼的士人，国外没有相与抗衡的邻国和外患的忧虑，反倒容易被灭亡。这样，就可以知道忧虑患难足以使人生存，安逸快乐足以使人灭亡的道理了。”

立贤无方。

《孟子·离娄下》

Promote men of virtue without regard to their class background.

无方： 没有固定的规矩。

孟子说："选择贤人不拘一格。"

凿斯池也，筑斯城也，与民守之，效死而民弗去，则是可为也。

《孟子·梁惠王下》

Your Highness should deepen the city moat and consolidate the city walls, and defend your kingdom together with the people. Your kingdom may survive if the people stand firm and are willing to sacrifice their lives to defend it.

这是孟子对滕文公说的话，滕文公问孟子："滕国是一个弱小的国家，处在齐国和楚国两个大国中间，我们是侍奉齐国呢，还是侍奉楚国呢?"孟子的主张是：为国当自立，不做大国的附庸。

孟子说："把护城河挖深，把城墙加固，和老百姓一道来保卫它，如果老百姓肯用生命来保卫国家，那就有希望了。"

故为政者，每人而悦之，日亦不足矣。

《孟子·离娄下》

The ruler would not have enough time to win everyone's favor.

子产治理郑国时，曾用自己所乘车子帮助老百姓渡河。孟子说："这不过是小恩小惠，其实他并不懂政治。如果提前把桥修好，老百姓就不会为渡河发愁了。执政者只要把国家治理好，他外出尽可以鸣锣开道，哪里用得着去帮助别人一个一个渡河呢?"

孟子说:"如果执政者去讨好每个人的欢心，那时间就太不够用了。"

民为贵，社稷次之，君为轻。

《孟子·尽心下》

To a state, the people are the most important thing, the altars to the gods of earth and grain come second, and the ruler is the least important thing.

社稷：古代帝王、诸侯所祭的土神和谷神。人非土不立，非谷不食，故封土立社，示有土也；稷，五谷之长，故立稷而祭之。历代封建王朝必先立社稷坛。灭亡一个国家后，必先变置该国的社稷。因后多以社稷为国家政权的标志。**民贵君轻：**孟子的政治主张，体现了先秦儒家民本主义思想。

孟子说："对一个国家来说，百姓最重要，社稷次之，君主为轻。"

乐民之乐者，民亦乐其乐；忧民之忧者，民亦忧其忧。乐以天下，忧以天下，然而不王者，未之有也。

《孟子·梁惠王下》

If a king takes his people's delights as his own delights, then his people will take his delights as their own; if a king takes his people's sorrows as his own sorrows, then his people will take his sorrows as their own. Any king who shares delights and sorrows with his people is sure to dominate the world.

孟子对齐宣王说:“如果国君以百姓的欢乐为自己的欢乐，百姓也会以国君的欢乐为自己的欢乐；国君以百姓的忧愁为自己的忧愁，百姓也会以国君的忧愁为自己的忧愁。和天下百姓同忧同乐的国君，就能使天下归服于他。”

保民而王，莫之能御也。

《孟子·梁惠王上》

No man can be prevented from unifying the world if he unifies it by making the lives of the people stable.

保民而王，莫之能御也：齐宣王问孟子：“您可以给我讲讲齐桓公、晋文公称霸诸侯的事吗?”孟子回答说：“孔子的学生们没有谈到过齐桓公、晋文公的事，所以没有传下来，我也不曾听说过。您如果一定让我说，我就说说用道德的力量统一天下的‘王道’吧!”齐宣王问：“要有什么样的道德才能统一天下呢?”孟子说了上面的话。

孟子说：“如果为着百姓们的生活安定而去统一天下，是没有人能够阻挡得了的。”

庖有肥肉，厩有肥马，民有饥色，野有饿莩，此率兽而食人也。兽相食，且人恶之；为民父母，行政，不免于率兽而食人，恶在其为民父母也？

《孟子·梁惠王上》

Now Your Highness has more than enough meat in you kitchen and more than enough strong horses in your stables. But your people look hungry and there are people who are starving to death by the roadsides. This is tantamount to the men in power leading animals to devour human beings. How can such men be officials?

厩：(jiù)，马栏，马厩。**且**：副词，“尚且”的意思。**恶**：(wū)，何也。这里作疑问副词用。

孟子对梁惠王说：“您现在厨房里有吃不完的肉，马厩里有用不完健壮的马匹，可是老百姓却面有饥色，路上有饿死的人，这就等于执政者领着禽兽来吃人。人们对禽兽间的自相残杀都感到厌恶，执政者却领着禽兽来吃人，这怎么能做老百姓的父母官呢？”

有恒产者有恒心，无恒产者无恒心。

《孟子·滕文公上》

People observe moral concepts and codes of behavior only when they have regular incomes from their property. If they do not have regular incomes they disregard morality.

有恒产者有恒心，无恒产者无恒心：恒产指土地、房屋、田园等不动产。恒心指持久不变的意志。孟子又说过“无恒产而有恒心者，惟士为能”的话（《孟子·梁惠王上》）。

孟子说：“有固定产业收入的人才可能有一定的道德观念和行为准则，没有固定产业收入的人就不会有一定的道德观念和行为准则。”

以万乘之国伐万乘之国，箪食壶浆，以迎王师，岂有他哉？避水火也。如水益深，如火益热，亦运而已矣。

《孟子·梁惠王下》

Qi attacked Yan, which was of the same strength, but the people of Yan welcomed the Qi army with wine and rice. This meant that they looked forward to liberation from the cruel rule of the king of Yan. But if the annexation brings more disasters to the people of Yan, it will be a change of form only, not content.

万乘之国：周制，王畿方千里，能出兵车万乘。战国后期，大诸侯国也有兵车万乘，“万乘之国七”（《战国策·序》），当时齐、燕均称“万乘之国”。**箪食壶浆**：箪(dān)，古代盛饭的竹器。浆，古代称以米熬成的汁，古人用以代酒。**王师**：帝王的军队，后多指正义之师。**水火**：喻灾难，艰难。

孟子说：“以齐国这样的大国去攻打同样强大的燕国，燕国的老百姓却送饭送酒欢迎您的军队，这没有别的意思，只不过他们盼望着早些脱离燕国统治者水深火热的统治罢了。如果齐国吞并燕国后，更加深了燕国百姓的灾难，那只不过是换汤不换药而已。”

上无道揆也，下无法守也，朝不信道，工不信度，君子犯义，小人犯刑，国之所存者幸也。

《孟子·离娄上》

If the ones high up hold no moral principles, then there will be no law for the ones low down. If the court does not believe in morality and justice, craftsmen will disregard the rules. If officials break the laws, then ordinary people will do the same. In this way, the state will be in danger.

上无道揆也：道揆，以义理度量事物。**下无法守也：**法守，按法度履行自己的职守。**朝：**朝廷。**工：**工匠。

孟子说“在上的没有道德规范，在下的就无法可依，朝廷不相信道义，工匠不相信尺度，官吏破坏法度，百姓就会触犯刑法，这样的国家就很危险了。”

桀纣之失天下也，失其民也；失其民者，失其心也。

《孟子·离娄上》

The reason Jie and Zhou failed to keep their empires is that they had lost the support and confidence of their people.

桀纣之失天下也：桀，夏朝最后一代王。嗜酒好声色，淫乐无度，滥杀谏臣，商汤趁机伐夏，夏亡。纣，商朝最后一代王。即位后重赋聚财，广建宫室，长夜饮乐，得妲己而唯言是从。重用谀臣，诛杀谏臣。后周武王会合各路诸侯代纣，纣死商亡。

孟子说："夏桀和商纣丧失天下的原因，是由于失去了百姓的支持，失去了民心。"

天下之本在国，国之本在家，家之本在身。

《孟子·离娄上》

Kingdoms are the basis of the empire, families are the basis of a kingdom and individuals are the basis of a family.

天下国家：孟子所说天下即指中国，国即指中国境内的各诸侯国。故儒家认为“身修而后家齐，家齐而后国治，国治而后天下平”（《礼记·大学》）。**本**：事物的根基和主体。

孟子说：“天下的基础是国，国的基础是家，家的基础是人。”

天下有道，小德役大德，小贤役大贤；天下无道，小役大，弱役强。

《孟子·离娄上》

When the world is in good order, people of low morality listen to people of high morality, and ordinary people listen to persons of virtue. When the world is in chaos, the powerful enslave the powerless, the strong enslave the weak.

小德役大德：意即“小德役于大德”“于”字省略。

孟子说：“国家政治清明，道德低的人听命于道德高的人，一般人听命于贤人。国家政治黑暗，力量大的奴役力量小的，强的奴役弱的。”

天时不如地利，地利不如人和。

《孟子·公孙丑下》

Favorable weather is less important than advantageous terrain, and advantageous terrain is less important than unity among the people.

天时、地利、人和： 天时、地利、人和是当时成语，而其内容时有所变。孟子在这里讲的天时是指阴晴寒暑之是否与攻战有利。地利则指高城深池、山川险阻。人和则指人心所向。

孟子说：“在战争中，天时不及地利重要，地利不及人和重要。”

域民不以封疆之界，固国不以山谿之险，威天下不以兵革之利。

《孟子·公孙丑下》

National border alone can not stop people from fleeing, precipitous terrain alone can not insure the security of the state, and force alone can not subjugate the world.

域：界限。**谿**：山谷。

孟子说：“单靠疆界不足以约束人民。单靠山川的险阻不足以保护国家的安全。单靠武力不足以威震天下。”

得道者多助，失道者寡助。寡助之至，亲戚畔之；多助之至，天下顺之。

《孟子·公孙丑下》

Practicing a policy of benevolence wins support from the people; otherwise the support of the people will be lost. If one loses the support of the people, even one's relatives will turn against one; if one wins the support of the people, all the people in the world will come to pledge allegiance

得道：得治国之道，即指行仁政。**亲戚：**古代对亲戚有多种解释，孟子所指父母兄弟姐妹而已。畔：同“叛”。

孟子说：“行仁政就得人心，不行仁政便失人心。失人心的结果，连亲戚都会背叛他；得人心的结果，天下的人都会归顺他。”

古之君子，其过也，如日月之食，民皆见之；及其更也，民皆仰之。今之君子，岂徒顺之，又从为之辞。

《孟子·公孙丑下》

The mistakes of ancient rulers were like solar and lunar eclipese—they were known to all people. After they corrected their mistakes, people admired them all the more. But a ruler now would not only leave the mistakes uncorrected, he would make excuses for them.

食：蚀。**仰之**：仰，指抬头看。此指日蚀月蚀复明而言，臣民对执政者改正错误，也正如盼望日月复明一样，故也说“仰之”。

孟子说：“古代的执政者，他的过错像日蚀月蚀一般挂在天上，老百姓都看得见。当他们改正以后，老百姓更加敬仰他们。今天的执政者，不仅将错就错，还一定要编造一番假道理来为错误辩护。”

明君制民之产，必使仰足以事父母，俯足以畜妻子，乐岁终身饱，凶年免于死亡；然后驱而之善，故民之从之也轻。

《孟子·梁惠王上》

A wise king would see to it that his people have enough wherewith to support their parents and to feed their wives and children, that they have enough food and clothes in years of good harvests, and do not perish in years of bad harvests. Then the people would listen when taught, and follow what is right.

乐岁：丰收之年。**凶年**：灾年。**驱**：驱使，逼迫。**轻**：轻易，容易。

孟子说："贤明的君主要使老百姓的产业收入上可以赡养父母，下足以抚养妻子儿女；好年成可以丰衣足食，坏年成也不至于饿死。然后再给他们讲从善的道理，老百姓自然就容易接受。"

贤者在位，能者在职；

《孟子·公孙丑上》

Employ virtuous persons as officials and assign capable persons to important posts.

贤者在位，能者在职：据朱熹等注解“贤者”和“能者”，“在位”和“在职”都有所区别。

孟子说：“使有德行和才能的人居于相当的官职。”

尧舜之道，不以仁政，不能平治天下。

《孟子·离娄上》

Even with Yao and Shun's statecraft, no one can dominate the world without policies of benevolence.

尧舜：唐尧和虞舜，远古部落联盟的首领。古史相传为圣明之君，孔子“祖述尧舜，宪章文武”（《礼记·中庸》），孟子“言必称尧舜”（《孟子·滕文公上》），都以尧舜并称。

孟子说：“即使有尧舜之道，如果不行仁政，也不能平治天下。”

不仁而得国者，有之矣；不仁而得天下者，未之有也。

《孟子·尽心下》

A ruler who is not benevolent can hold onto a state. But no man who is not benevolent can rule the world.

国：指当时的诸侯国。天下：指全中国。

孟子说："不行仁道而能得到一国之政的，有这样的事；不行仁道而能得到天下的，这样的事却不曾有过。"

春秋无义战。彼善於此，则有之矣。征者，上伐下也，敌国不相征也。

《孟子·尽心下》

There were no just wars in the Spring and Autumn Period. Only some kings were better than others, and senior states could send punitive expeditions against states of lower status, but states of the same status could not send punitive expeditions against one another.

春秋无义战：春秋，时代名。孔子《春秋》纪事，从鲁隐公元年至哀公十四年（公元前722—前481年）共二百四十二年，称为春秋时代。今以周平王东迁至韩赵魏三家分晋（公元前770年—前476年）共二百九十五年，为春秋时代。**上伐下**：孔子说："天下有道，则礼乐征伐自天子出；天下无道，则礼乐征伐自诸侯出。"**敌国**：同等级的国家。

孟子说："春秋时代没有正义战争。有的君主比别的国家的君主好一些是有的。但征伐，只能是上级讨伐下级，同等级的国家是不能互相征伐的。所以说春秋无义战。"

天下溺，援之以道；嫂溺，援之以手——子欲手援天下乎？

《孟子·离娄上》

If all the people of the world are drowning, they are to be saved by means of the Way. A drowning sister-in-law is to be saved with the hand. Do you expect me to save all the people in the world with my hand?

天下溺，援之以道：孟子决定离开齐国，齐王派淳于髡去挽留孟子，淳于髡问："男女之间，授受不亲，这是礼制吗？"孟子回答说："是礼制。"淳于髡说："那么，假如眼看着嫂嫂掉到水里，可以用手去拉她吗？"孟子说："看见嫂嫂掉到水里，不去拉她，这简直是豺狼。男女之间授受不亲，这是常礼。看见嫂嫂掉到水里，用手去救她，这是变通的办法。"淳于髡说："现在天下人都掉在了水里，您不去救援，又是什么缘故呢？"孟子说了上面的话。

孟子说："天下人都掉在水里了，要用'道'去援救；嫂嫂掉在水里，用手去援救——你难道要我用一双手去援救天下人吗？"

尊贤使能，俊杰在位。

《孟子·公孙丑上》

A king should respect virtuous persons, employ capable persons and put outstanding persons in posts so as to give full play to their wisdom and capabilities.

贤能：贤良有才能之人。**俊杰：**朱熹《孟子集注》云："俊杰，才德之异于众者。"

孟子说："尊重有道德的人，重用有才能的人，使杰出的人物都有发挥才干的机会。"

君子之泽五世而斩，小人之泽五世而斩。

《孟子·离娄下》

The influence of a gentleman on posterity lasts five generations only, as does that of a petty man.

君子之泽，小人之泽：有人以大德大凶解君子小人。也有以“君子为圣贤在位者，小人为圣贤不在位者”解“君子小人”。**泽：**朱熹《孟子集注》曰：“犹言流风余韵也。”可理解为“影响”。**斩：**断绝，消失。

孟子说：“君子对后世的影响五代以后就会衰亡，小人对后世的影响五代以后也会消失。”

交友篇

On Friends

友也者，友其德也。

《孟子·万章下》

When one befriends others, what he should take into consideration is the others' good qualities and not other things.

友其德：这是孟子关于交友及朋友之间交往的原则。孔子主张"以文会友，以友辅仁"（《论语·颜渊》），孟子主张"友其德"，即"不挟长、不挟贵、不挟兄弟而友"（《孟子·万章下》），孟子认为朋友之间"责善，朋友之道也"（《孟子·离娄下》）。

孟子说："交朋友，是看中朋友的品德而交。"

有不虞之誉，有求全之毁。

《孟子·离娄上》

There is unexpected praise and highly demanding censure.

不虞： 虞（yú），意料，料度。不虞，没有料到。**求全之毁：** 求全，希求完美无缺。朱熹《孟子集注》：“求免于毁而反致毁，是为求全之毁。”后谓一心想保全声誉，反而受到诋毁。

孟子说：“有意想不到的赞誉，也有过于苛求的诋毁。”

听其言也，观其眸子，人焉廋哉？

《孟子·离娄上》

Look straight into a man's eyes while listening to his words, and he won't be able to conceal what is in his mind.

眸子：眸（móu），本指瞳人，泛指眼睛。**廋**：（sōu），隐藏。孟子认为：观察一个人，没有比观察他的眼睛更准确了。因为眼睛不能掩盖一个人的丑恶。心正，则眼睛明亮；心不正，则目不明。

孟子说："听一个人说话的时候，注意观察他的眼睛，这个人的善恶是无法隐藏的。"

人之易其言也，无责耳矣。

《孟子·离娄上》

Those who indulge themselves in verbiage will have no achievements.

易：去声，轻易也。**无责耳矣：**不足责备。

孟子说："夸夸其谈的人，不足以任大事。"

君子不亮，恶乎执？

《孟子·告子下》

How can a gentleman have friends if he is not honest and does not keep his word?

亮：同“谅”，诚信。**执**：朋友，至交。

孟子说：“君子不讲诚信，如何能有朋友？”

人必自侮，然后人侮之；家必自毁，而后人毁之；国必自伐，而后人伐之。

《孟子·离娄上》

A person can only be insulted when his own behavior invites insults; a family will be destroyed only when it has destroyed itself beforehand, and a kingdom will be invaded only when it provides a cause.

孟子说："人必先有遭侮辱的行为，才会遭别人侮辱；家必先有毁坏的因素，外力才能毁坏它；国必先有被讨伐的原因，才会被别国讨伐。"

自暴者，不可与有言也；自弃者，不可与有为也。

《孟子·离娄上》

One may not converse with someone who does violence to himself, and one may not co-operate with someone who has abandoned himself.

自暴、自弃： 暴，损害，糟蹋。自己糟蹋自己，自己瞧不起自己，形容一种自卑自贱，甘居落后的心理。成语“自暴自弃”即源于此。**有言、有为：** 有言，有益的话。有为，有所作为。

孟子说：“和糟蹋自己的人，谈不出什么有益的话；和瞧不起自己的人，干不成什么大事。”

不挟长，不挟贵，不挟兄弟而友。

《孟子·万章下》

The principle (of friendship) is not to take advantage of one's seniority or high position or the high positions of one's relatives.

挟：(xié)，倚仗，恃以自重。“不挟长，不挟贵，不挟兄弟”是孟子教导弟子交友的原则。他认为：“交朋友，是看中朋友的品德而交，心中就不存在有任何依仗的观念。”(《孟子·万章下》)

孟子说：“交朋友不依仗自己年纪大，不依仗自己地位高，不依仗自己兄弟的富贵。”

教育篇

On Education

得天下英才而教育之，三乐也。

《孟子·尽心上》

The third delight of a gentleman is that he can gather together all the talented people in the world and instruct them.

英才： 才智出众的人。

孟子说："能够聚会天下才智出众的人进行教育，也是人生一大乐事。"

大匠不为拙工改废绳墨，羿不为拙射变其彀率。

《孟子·尽心上》

A master craftsman would not change his tools just to make things easier for clumsy workers. Yi would not change his rules of archery for the sake of poor marksmen.

绳墨：木匠以绳濡墨打直线的工具，喻称规矩或法度。**彀率**：弓弩张开的程度。

孟子说："高明的工匠不因工人笨拙而改变或废弃规矩，羿也不因射手拙劣而改变拉弓的标准。"

大匠诲人必以规矩，学者亦必以规矩。

《孟子·告子上》

Great carpenters, when teaching their craft, used compasses and squares, and their students followed suit.

必以规矩：孟子这里说的“必以规矩”是防止创述异端邪说的意思。

孟子说：“好的木匠教徒弟，一定依循规矩；学习的人也一定要依循规矩。”

山径之蹊，间介然用之而成路；为间不用，则茅塞之矣。

《孟子·尽心下》

A narrow mountain path will be broadened into a road if trodden frequently, but it will be overgrown with grass if not used for a long period of time.

山径：山间小路。**蹊：**（xī），小路。**介然：**专一，坚定不移。**间：**（jiān），一定的空间或时间里。

孟子说："山间的小路只一点宽，经常有人走就会越来越宽。只要一段时间没人走，又会被野草堵塞了。"

古者易子而教之，父子之间不责善。责善则离，离则不祥莫大焉。

《孟子·离娄上》

In ancient times gentlemen exchanged sons to educate them, in order to avoid mutual blaming. Mutual blaming would lead to estrangement, which is the worst thing in the world.

易子而教：古人往往互相交换儿子来教育。也就是公孙丑所问的问题，“君子为什么不亲自教育自己的儿子”。
祥：善。

孟子说：“古时候君子往往互相交换儿子来教育，使父子间避免发生冲突，父子间发生冲突，就容易产生隔阂，父子间产生隔阂，是君子最伤脑筋的事。”

中也养不中，才也养不才，故人乐有贤父兄也。

《孟子·离娄下》

Men of lofty morality should educate and influence men of doubtful morality; men of talent should educate and influence untalented men. For everyone delights in having a talented and highly moral superior.

中也养不中，才也养不才：朱熹《孟子集注》："无过不及之谓中，足以有为之谓才；养，谓涵育薰陶，俟其自化也。"中，即中庸，儒家认为做人的标准。

孟子说："道德高尚的人来教育影响道德不高的人，才能高的人来教育影响才能低下的人，所以每个人都希望有个才德高尚的长者。"

人之有道也，饱食、煖衣、逸居而无教，则近于禽兽。

《孟子·滕文公上》

Human beings would not be far from animals and birds if they had only enough food to eat, enough clothes to wear and enough shelter but no education.

人之有道也： 有，为也。有道，为道。**煖：** （xuān），温暖。

孟子说："人之所以为人，只是吃饱穿暖，住得安逸了是远远不够的，如果没有教育，也就和禽兽没什么差别了。"

羿之教人射，必志于彀。

《孟子·告子上》

Yi, in teaching archery, stressed drawing the bow to its full, and his students followed suit.

必志于彀：彀，弓满也。孟子这里说的“必志于彀”是防止半途而废的意思。

孟子说：“羿教人射箭，一定拉满弓；学习的人也一定要拉满弓。”

仁言不如仁声之入人深也，善政不如善教之得民也。善政，民畏之；善教，民爱之。善政得民财，善教得民心。

《孟子·尽心上》

Benevolent words do not strike root in the heart of people as much as benevolent music does. Good government does not win the hearts of the people as much as good education does. People fear good government, but they love good education. Good government can obtain the wealth created by the people, but good education can win the hearts of the people.

仁言：仁德的话。**仁声**：仁德的音乐。指古代乐曲《雅》、《颂》的演奏声。**善政**：良好的政治。**善教**：良好的教育。**善政，民畏之；善教，民爱之**：赵岐注曰："畏之，不逋怠，故赋役举而财聚于一家也；爱之，乐风化而上下亲，故欢心可得也。"**民财**：老百姓创造的财富。

孟子说："仁德的话不如仁德的音乐深入人心；良好的政治不如良好的教育容易获得民心。良好的政治，百姓畏惧它；良好的教育，百姓爱它。良好的政治能得到百姓创造的财富，良好的教育能得到百姓的心。"

教亦多术矣，予不屑之教诲也者，是亦教诲之而已矣。

《孟子·告子下》

There are many ways of teaching. To neglect purposely to teach is also a way of teaching.

术：方法。不屑：表示轻视。

孟子说："教育有很多种方法，我故意冷落他，促使他发愤，这也是一种教诲的方法。"

君子之所以教者五：有如时雨化之者，有成德者，有达财者，有答问者，有私淑艾者。此五者，君子之所以教也。

《孟子·尽心上》

There are, for a gentleman, five ways of teaching: by influencing like moistening with rain and dew, by promoting virtue, by cultivating talent, by answering inquiries, and by encouraging self-cultivation. These are the five ways of teaching.

财：同“材”。**私淑艾**：淑、艾同义。犹“私淑”也。

孟子说：“君子的教育方法有五种：有像雨露滋润万物的，有促成人品德的，有培养人才能的，有解答疑问的，还有鼓励人自学的。这是君子育人的五种方法。”

梓匠轮舆能与人规矩，不能使人巧。

《孟子·尽心下》

A skilled craftsman can pass on his techniques to others, but he cannot make others skillful.

梓匠轮舆：梓匠，木工。轮舆：轮人和舆人。轮人指制造车轮的匠人；舆人指制造车厢的匠人。

孟子说："高明的工匠可以把制作工艺传授给人，却不能使人具有高明的技巧。"

贤者以其昭昭使人昭昭，今以其昏昏使人昭昭。

《孟子·尽心下》

Virtuous men, in instructing others, get themselves enlightened first, and then try to enlighten others with their enlightenment. But nowadays those who try to enlighten others are unenlightened themselves.

昭昭：明白。**昏昏**：糊涂的样子。

孟子说："贤者教导别人必先自己明白，然后才要求别人明白；今为人师者，自己还不明白，却用这些模模糊糊的东西要求别人明白。"

富岁，子弟多赖；凶岁，子弟多暴，非天之降才尔殊也，其所以陷溺其心者然也。

《孟子·告子上》

In good years young men tend to be lazy while in bad years they tend to be violent. But this is not due to difference in their natures; it is due to changes in their natures caused by their environment.

富岁、凶岁：丰年、灾年。**赖**：懒。**暴**：强暴。**才**：资质。

孟子说："丰收年成，少年子弟多半懒惰；灾荒年成，少年子弟多半强暴。这不是天生资质有这样的不同，是由于环境使他们的本性改变的缘故。"

上无礼，下无学，贼民兴，丧无日矣。

《孟子·离娄上》

A state will inevitably fall if those high up ignore propriety and righteousness, and those low down are uneducated and undisciplined persons who violate the laws.

上无礼：在上位的人没有道德规范。**下无学：**老百姓不受教育。

孟子说："如果执政者没有礼义，老百姓不受教育，违法乱纪的人都起来了，那国家也就要灭亡了。"

天下不心服而王者，未之有也。

《孟子·离娄下》

One can never unify the world if the hearts of all the people are not won over.

天下不心服而王者：孟子的意思是：如果用仁义礼智使人屈服是办不到的，如果用仁义礼智去教育人，却能使人心服，只有使天下人心服才能统一天下，从来没有天下人心不服而能统一天下的。

孟子说：“从来没有天下人心不服而能统一天下的。”

言近而指远者，善言也；守约而施博者，善道也。

《孟子·尽心下》

Simple words with far-reaching meaning are good words. Principles easy to practice with good effects are good principles.

言近：言语浅近，易于接受。**指远**：深远。**守约**：掌握要领，操持简单。**施博**：广大。

孟子说："言语浅近，意义却深远的，是善言；操作简单，效果却广大的，是善道。"

君子引而不发，跃如也。

《孟子·尽心上》

A gentleman trains others in the way Yi taught archery. He drew bows without discharging the arrow, just to show his eagerness to shoot.

引而不发，跃如也：引，拉弓。发，射箭。拉满了弓，却不发箭，作出跃跃欲试的样子。成语“引而不发”源于此，后比喻作好准备，待机行事。也常用以比喻善于启发引导学生或善于控制自己。

孟子说：“君子育人就像教人射箭一样，拉满了弓，却不发箭，作出跃跃欲试的样子。”

仁义篇

On Benevolence and Justice

仁人无敌于天下

《孟子·尽心下》

A benevolent man has no rival in the world.

仁人：行仁政的人，指周武王。

孟子说："仁人天下无敌"。

亲亲，仁也；敬长，义也；无他，达之天下也。

《孟子·尽心上》

To love one's parents is benevolence and to respect one's elder brother is righteousness. Only these two virtues, benevolence and righteousness, are universal virtues.

仁、义：孟子提出"仁，人心也；义，人路也"（《孟子·告子上》）这种以心释仁，以义行仁的原则确立了孟子在儒学传统中的地位。

孟子说："爱亲为仁，敬长为义，只有仁和义是通达天下的两种品德。"

君子之于物也，爱之而弗仁；于民也，仁之而弗亲。

《孟子·尽心上》

A gentleman needs to take good care of all things, but needs not treat them with benevolence. He should treat people with benevolence only, and not with affection.

弗：不，不可，不必。

孟子说："君子对于物，只知道爱惜就够了，而不必以仁德对待它；对于百姓，只应以仁德对待他们而并不必表示亲爱。"

仁也者，人也。合而言之，道也。

《孟子·尽心下》

To be benevolent is to be human. The joining of the two means principles.

仁者人也：古音“仁”与“人”相同。《说文》曰：“仁，亲也。从人二。”意思是只要有两个人在一起，就不能不有仁的道德，而仁的道德也只能在人与人之间产生。《礼记·中庸》也有“仁者，人也”。

孟子说：“仁的意思就是人，仁和人合在一起说，就是道。”

一正君而国定矣。

《孟子·离娄上》

When rulers' errors are corrected their kingdoms will be stable.

孟子说：“君主仁，没有人不仁。君主义，没有人不义。君主正，没有人不正。”（《孟子·离娄上》）

孟子说：“只要君主端正了，国家就安定了。”

惟仁者为能以大事小，是故汤事葛，文王事昆夷。惟智者为能以小事大，故太王事獯鬻，勾践事吴。

《孟子·梁惠王下》

A benevolent person would serve the weak even though he is strong. So Tang of Shang served Count Ge and King Wen served Kun Yi. A wise man would serve the strong if he is weak. So King Tai served Xun Yu and Gou Jian served Fu Chai.

汤事葛：汤，商王朝的建立者，亦称成汤。葛，古国名，嬴姓，故城在今河南省宁陵县北十五里，后为汤所灭。汤灭葛之前商汤曾服事葛伯。**文王事昆夷：**文王，周王朝的建立者，即周文王。昆夷亦作混夷，周初的西戎国名。文王事昆夷的详情已不可考。**太王事獯鬻：**太王亦作大王，即古公亶父，古代周族领袖，周文王祖父。獯鬻亦作薰育。当时北方少数民族。**勾践事吴：**越王勾践被吴王夫差打败，逃到会稽山，卑辞厚礼向吴国求和，自己为吴王当马前卒。后终于报仇，灭了吴国。

孟子说：“仁德的人可以以大事小，所以商汤曾服事葛伯，文王曾服事昆夷。聪明的人可以以小事大，所以太王曾服事獯鬻，勾践曾服事夫差。”

大人者，不失其赤子之心者也。

《孟子·离娄下》

A man of virtue is one who has a heart as innocent as that of a new-born baby.

不失其赤子之心：赵岐《孟子注》曰："大人谓君，国君视民当如赤子，不失其民心之谓也。"此说未必可信，"大人"也未必专指"国君"，此处指"有德之人"似更贴切。赤子，指初生的婴儿。赤子之心，比喻纯洁的心。

孟子说："道德高尚的人就是能保持纯洁善良之心的人。"

大人者，言不必信，行不必果，惟义所在。

《孟子·离娄下》

A man of virtue need not keep his word and act resolutely all the time so long as all his words and actions conform to the right course.

言不必信，行不必果：《论语·子路》：“言必信，行必果”的话是孔子称最下一等的“士”就能做到的，所以这里孟子说“大人者，言不必信，行不必果”。

孟子说：“有德行的人，说话不一定句句守信，行为不一定事事决断，其言行只要符合义就行。”

仁者无敌。

《孟子·梁惠王上》

He who practices benevolence is invincible!

孟子对梁惠王说：“执政者行仁政将无敌于天下。”

民之归仁也，犹水之就下、兽之走圹也。故为渊驱鱼者，獭也；为丛驱爵者，鹯也；为汤武驱民者，桀与纣也。

《孟子·离娄上》

People will submit to policies of benevolence as water flows downhill and animals gather in deserted land and forests. Just as the otter drives fish into deep ponds and the eagle drives birds into the forests, so Jie of the Xia Dynasty and Zhou of the Shang Dynasty drove the people into the arms of Tand of Shang Dynasty and King Wu of the Zhou Dynasty.

獭：(tǎ)，水獭。爵：同“雀”。鹯：(zhān)，一种猛禽，一说鹞鹰。

孟子说：“百姓归附于仁政，好像水往低处流，野兽向旷野山林一样自然。所以，把鱼赶入深池的是水獭，把鸟雀赶入树林的是鹞鹰，把百姓赶到商汤、周武王一边的正是夏桀和商纣。”

仁则荣，不仁则辱；今恶辱而居不仁，是犹恶湿而居下也。

《孟子·公孙丑上》

Practicing a policy of benevolence leads to glory; otherwise humiliation occurs. Nowadays, although men in power detest humiliation, they do not practice a policy of benevolence. This is like detesting moisture but living in low-lying land.

仁则荣，不仁则辱：指诸侯以及卿相而言，这两句省略了主语。**居不仁：**行为不仁。

孟子说："如果实行仁政，就会得到荣耀；如果不行仁政，就会遭受屈辱。如今的执政者，都不想遭受屈辱但又不肯行仁政，这好比厌恶潮湿却又自居于低洼之地一样。"

君子之言也，不下带而道存焉；君子之守，修其身而天下平。

《孟子·尽心下》

Even when a gentleman talks about daily affairs, principles lie within his words. A gentleman begins with self-cultivation, but he can make the whole world peaceful.

不下带：带，束腰之带，朱熹《孟子集注》：“古人视不下于带，则带之上乃目前常见至近之处也。举目前之近事，而至理存焉。”

孟子说：“君子的言语，讲的虽是日常所见的事情，可‘道’就在其中；君子的操守从修养自身开始，从而使天下太平。”

仁之实，事亲是也；义之实，从兄是也；智之实，知斯二者弗去是也；礼之实，节文斯二者是也；乐之实，乐斯二者，乐则生矣。

《孟子·离娄上》

The core of benevolence is to be filial to one's parents; the core of righteousness is to yield to one's elder brothers; the core of wisdom is to know the meaning of benevolence and righteousness and adhere to them steadfastly; the core of propriety is to regulate and adjust the relations between benevolence and righteousness; the core of happiness is the enjoyment of practicing benevolence and righteousness.

实：指实际内容，和“名”相对。**亲**：父母。**从**：(cóng)，听从，顺从。**斯**：此，这。**弗**：不，不可。

孟子说：“仁的核心是孝顺父母；义的核心是顺从兄长；智的核心是明白仁和义的道理而坚持不懈；礼的核心是能对仁和义加以调节和修饰；乐的核心是能从实行仁和义中得到快乐。”

执中无权，犹执一也。所恶执一者，为其贼道也，举一而废百也。

《孟子·尽心上》

To adhere to the middle way without being flexible is being stubbornly biased. Why should I detest stubborn bias? Because it hurts the way of benevolence and righteousness. It sticks to one point without taking other points into account.

执中：中庸之道，称作事无过无不及为执中。**权**：变通，机变。**执一**：固执不变。**贼**：伤害，损害，败坏。

孟子说："主张中庸如果不知变通，便是偏执。为什么厌恶偏执呢？因为它损害仁义之道，只是执其一点而不顾其余。"

三代之得天下也以仁，其失天下也以不仁。国之所以废兴存亡者亦然。

《孟子·离娄上》

The three dynasties, Xia, Shang and Zhou, could dominate the world because they all practiced policies of benevolence, and they lost their empires because they all discarded policies of benevolence. The prosperity and decay of kingdoms also follow this rule.

三代：夏、商、周。孟子认为天子不仁，便不能保天下；诸侯不仁，便不能保国家；卿大夫不仁，便不能保封地；士人和老百姓不仁，便不能保自身。现在有些人怕死，却又不仁，这好比怕醉却偏要喝酒一样。

孟子说：“夏、商、周三代以仁得天下，以不仁失天下。国家的兴盛和衰亡也是这个道理。”

仁之胜不仁也，犹水胜火。

《孟子·告子上》

Benevolence can overcome cruelty, as water can extinguish fire.

水胜火：水可以灭火。孟子说：“今天所谓行仁的人，好像用一杯水来扑灭一车柴的大火，火不能灭，便说水不能灭火，也就不再相信仁胜过不仁的道理。于是这些人又和不仁的人走在了一起，结果连他们已行的一点仁也消失了。”（《孟子·告子上》）

孟子说：“仁胜过不仁，正像水可以灭火一样。”

仁，人之安宅也；义，人之正路也。旷安宅而弗居，舍正路而不由，哀哉！

《孟子·离娄上》

Benevolence is where one should reside; justice is the right road along which one should go. It is a pity to refuse to reside where one should reside and depart from the road one should follow!

安宅：安居。孟子认为仁是人的安宅。**正路：**大路。

孟子说："仁是人应居之处，义是人之正路。舍应居之处不居，舍正道不走，乃是人之悲哀。"

恻隐之心，人皆有之；羞恶之心，人皆有之；恭敬之心，人皆有之；是非之心，人皆有之。

《孟子·告子上》

Compassion is common to all; so are the senses of shame, respect, and right and wrong.

恻隐之心：孟子指一种天赋的同情心，他还认为同情心是“仁”的萌芽。**羞恶之心**：孟子指一种天赋的羞耻心，又认为羞耻心是“义”的萌芽。**恭敬之心**：孟子指一种天赋的谦让心，又称“辞让之心”。又认为辞让心是“礼”的萌芽。**是非之心**：孟子指一种天赋的分辨是非之心，这种天生分辨是非的能力是“智”的萌芽。

孟子说：“同情心，每个人都有；羞耻心，每个人都有；恭敬心，每个人都有；是非心，每个人都有。”

恻隐之心，仁也；羞恶之心，义也；恭敬之心，礼也；是非之心，智也，仁义礼智，非由外铄我也。我固有之也，弗思耳矣。

《孟子·告子上》

Compassion gives rise to benevolence, a sense of shame to righteousness, respect to propriety, and sense of right and wrong to wisdom. Benevolence, righteousness, propriety and wisdom are not endowed by others, but are inborn; it is just that one has not reflected upon them.

铄：消损，毁损。

孟子说："同情心属于仁，羞耻心属于义，恭敬心属于礼，是非心属于智。这仁义礼智，不是由外人给我的，而是我本来就有的，不过不曾认真想罢了。"

人性之善也，犹水之就下也。

《孟子·告子上》

Human nature tends toward good, just as water tends to flow downward.

性善：孔子说："性相近也，习相远也。"（《论语·阳货》）孟子是主张"人性善"的（见《孟子·公孙丑上》），但在中国哲学史上也有人认为"人之性恶，其善者伪也"（《荀子·性恶》），而王充则认为人性有恶有善。

孟子说："人性本善，就像水向低处流一样。"

声闻过情，君子耻之。

《孟子·离娄下》

A gentleman is ashamed of his reputation surpassing his qualities.

声闻：名声，名誉。孟子弟子徐辟说："孔子曾数次称赞水，说'水呀，水呀！'他到底称赞水什么呢？"孟子说："有源之水汩汩而流，昼夜不停，漫过坎地，奔流向前，一直注入海洋。孔子就是赞扬水之有源这一点。假如是无源之水，一到雨季就沟渠盈满，但很快就干枯了。"孟子以无源之水喻名不副实。

孟子说："君子以名不副实为耻。"

以善服人者，未有能服人者也；以善养人，然后能服天下。

《孟子·离娄下》

One can never convince others with truth, but all the world will be convinced if one educates the world with truth.

善：孟子本意指仁义礼智，在这里可理解为真理。**养**：教养。

孟子说："以善服人，没有能使人服从的。以善教人，能使天下人归服。"

君仁，莫不仁；君义，莫不义；君正，莫不正。

《孟子·离娄上》

If rulers are benevolent, then all their people will be benevolent too. If rulers are righteous, then all their people will be righteous also. If rulers are upright, all their people will be upright also.

孟子说："君主仁，没有人不仁。君主义，没有人不义。君主正，没有人不正。"

人之有德慧术知者，恒存乎疢疾。

《孟子·尽心上》

Men acquire virtue, wisdom, capability and talent in adversity.

德慧术知：道德、聪明、本领、才能。**疢疾**：疢(chèn)，灾祸，忧患。

孟子说：“人之所以有道德、聪明、本领、才能，常常存在于忧患之中。”

仁，人心也；义，人路也。舍其路而弗由，放其心而不知求，哀哉！

《孟子·告子上》

Benevolence is the heart of a man, righteousness the road. How sad it is one should depart from the right road and not seek the heart that has gone astray, alas!

由：从，自。弗由，不走，不从这条路上走。**放心：**放，丢失，走失。

孟子说："仁是人的心，义是人的路。放弃正路而不走，丧失了善良之心不知寻找，可悲呀！"

生亦我所欲，所欲有甚于生者，故不为苟得也；死亦我所恶，所恶有甚于死者，故患有所不辟也。

《孟子·告子上》

Though life is what I treasure, there is something that is more precious to me, and that is righteousness. So I will not draw on an ignoble existence. Death is what I detest, but there is something that I detest more than death, and that is unrighteousness. So I will not adopt the attitude of avoiding disasters.

苟：随便。辟：同“避”。

孟子说：“生命虽然是我所宝贵的，但对我来说还有比生命更为宝贵的，那就是义。所以我不做苟且偷生的事。死亡是我所厌恶的，但还有比死亡更为我所厌恶的，那就是不义。所以我不会对一切祸患都取躲避的态度。”

鱼，我所欲也，熊掌亦我所欲也；二者不可得兼，舍鱼而取熊掌者也。生亦我所欲也，义亦我所欲也；二者不可得兼，舍生而取义者也。

《孟子·告子上》

Fish is what I want and bear's paw is also what I want. If I cannot have both, I prefer bear's paw to fish. Life is what I treasure and righteousness is also what I treasure. If I cannot have both, I prefer righteousness to life.

孟子说："鱼是我喜欢吃的，熊掌也是我喜欢吃的，如果两者不能同时得到，我便会舍鱼而取熊掌。生命是我所宝贵的，义也是我所宝贵的。如果两者发生矛盾，必须舍弃一种时，我便会牺牲生命，而取义。"

仁者爱人，有礼者敬人。爱人者，人恒爱之；敬人者，人恒敬之。

《孟子·离娄下》

A benevolent person loves others and a polite man respects others. The ones who love others will always be loved by others and the one who respect others will always be respected by others.

恒：长久，经常。

孟子说："仁人爱人，有礼的人懂得恭敬别人。爱别人的人，别人也会爱他。懂得恭敬别人的人，别人也会恭敬他。"

君子所以异于人者，以其存心也。君子以仁存心，以礼存心。

《孟子·离娄下》

A gentleman differs from ordinary people in that he has different ideas in his mind. What he has in his mind is benevolence and the rites.

存心：居心，心里想的。

孟子说："君子和一般人不同的地方，就在于心里想的不一样。君子心里想的是仁，是礼。"

居天下之广居，立天下之正位，行天下之大道。

《孟子·滕文公下》

（As for males）the guiding principle should be benevolence. His performance should conform to the rites and his behavior should be righteous and just.

广居：天下最宽广的居处——仁。**正位：**天下最正确的位置——礼。**大道：**天下最宽广的路——义。”

孟子说：“（至于男子）应居之以仁，立之以礼，行之以义。”

孝亲篇

On Filial Piety and Fraternal Duty

父母俱存，兄弟无故，一乐也。

《孟子·尽心上》

The first delight of a gentleman is that his parents are hale and hearty, and his brothers are safe and sound.

故：灾害，丧亡。

孟子说："父母健在，兄弟平安，是人生第一种快乐。"

老吾老，以及人之老；幼吾幼，以及人之幼。

《孟子·梁惠王上》

Extend your respect for your aged parents to all the aged, and extend your love for your own children to all children.

老吾老，以及人之老：现在的社会只提“尊老”而不提“孝亲”，现在很多年轻人不孝敬父母，甚至不赡养父母。一个连自己父母都不孝敬的人，会尊敬别人的老人吗？

孟子说：“由尊敬自己的老人，从而推广到尊敬所有的老人；爱护自己的儿女，从而推广到爱护所有人家的儿女。”

人人亲其亲、长其长，而天下平。

《孟子·离娄下》

If one loves his parents and respects his seniors, the world will be at peace.

亲其亲、长其长：亲爱自己的亲人，恭敬自己的长辈。

孟子说："只要人人能亲爱自己的双亲，尊敬自己的长辈，天下就会太平。"

亲亲而仁民，仁民而爱物。

《孟子·尽心上》

A gentleman shows affection for his kin, benevolence toward other people and care for all other things.

亲亲：爱自己的父母、亲人。**仁民：**以仁德对待百姓。**爱物：**爱惜万物。

孟子说："君子亲爱亲人，因而能仁爱百姓；仁爱百姓，因而能爱惜万物"

养生者不足以当大事，惟送死可以当大事。

To support and wait upon parents is not a major task. But the burial of parents is a major task.

养生送死： 孟子是很重视为父母送终的，而且说过："君子不以天下俭其亲。" 他以"士"礼葬父，以"大夫"礼葬母曾受人诽谤，而他终不悔。其实，"厚葬无益于死者"，孔子主张"生，事之以礼；死，葬之以礼"（《论语·为政》）和孟子"养生送死"的观点有所不同。

孟子说："供养父母生活算不得什么大事，只有为父母送终才算一件大事。"

世俗所谓不孝者五，惰其四支，不顾父母之养，一不孝也；博弈好饮酒，不顾父母之养，二不孝也；好货财，私妻子，不顾父母之养，三不孝也；从耳目之欲，以为父母戮，四不孝也；好勇斗很，以危父母，五不孝也。

《孟子·离娄下》

Five kinds of behavior are commonly called unfilial. The first one is laziness, disregarding one's duty to support one's parents. The second is indulgence in drinking and playing chess, disregarding one's duty to support one's parents. The third is to be a money grabber and dote on one's wife and children only, disregarding one's duty to support one's parents. The fourth is to be addicted to music and fond of women, bringing humiliation on one's parents. The fifth is to take to fighting, endangering one's parents.

四支：四肢。**博奕**：六博和围棋。六博，古代一种博戏，共十二棋六黑六白，两人相博，每人六棋，故名。**私**：偏爱，偏私。**从**：同“纵”。**戮**：侮辱，罪责。**很**：今作“狠”字。**五不孝**：孟子在《离娄上》篇中还说过：“不孝有三，无后为大”的话。赵岐注云：“于礼有不孝者三者，谓阿意曲从，陷亲不义，一不孝也；家贫亲老，不为禄仕，二不孝也；不娶无子，绝先祖祀，三不孝也。”

孟子说：“一般人所说的不孝有五：四肢不勤，不顾父母生活，一不孝；好下棋饮酒，不顾父母生活，二不孝；好钱财，偏爱妻室儿女，不顾父母生活，三不孝；好声色，父母因此而受辱，四不孝；逞勇好斗，累及父母，五不孝。”

不得乎亲，不可以为人；不顺乎亲，不可以为子。

《孟子·离娄上》

A man cannot be called a man if he fails to win favor from his parents; a son cannot be called a son if he fails to submit to his parents' will.

不得乎亲：不能得到父母的欢心。**不顺乎亲**：不能顺从父母的心意。

孟子说："不能得到父母的欢心，不可以做人；不能顺从父母的旨意，不可以做儿子。"

事，孰为大？事亲为大；守，孰为大？守身为大。

《孟子·离娄上》

Whom should be served first? Parents should be served first. What should be kept first? Moral integrity should be kept first.

事：侍奉。**孰：**谁。**守：**守护，守卫。**守身：**洁身自爱，使不为外物所移。

孟子说："侍奉谁最重要？侍奉父母最重要。守护什么最重要？守护自己的节操最重要。"

悦亲有道，反身不诚，不悦于亲矣。

《孟子·离娄上》

To please one's parents, one should serve them with sincerity. How can he please his parents if he is insincere when he reflects on himself?

悦亲：悦，喜欢；亲，父母。取得父母的欢心。**反身**：儒家一种重要修养方法，指通过反省来检验自己的思想和行为是否符合道德标准。

孟子说："要使父母满意，首先侍奉父母要心诚。反躬自责，若自己心意不诚，又怎能使父母满意呢？"

图书在版编目（CIP）数据

孟子名言录/蔡希勤编注：何祚康，郁苓译．北京：华语教学出版社，2002.1

ISBN 7－80052－806－5

Ⅰ．孟…　Ⅱ．①蔡…　②何…　③郁…　Ⅲ．英语－对照读物，格言－英、汉　Ⅳ．H319.4：B

中国版本图书馆 CIP 数据核字（2001）第 083450 号

孟子名言录

编注　蔡希勤
英译　何祚康　郁　苓
绘图　李士伋

*

华语教学出版社出版
（中国北京百万庄大街 24 号）
邮政编码　100037
电话　（86）10－68995871
　　　（86）10－68326333
传真　（86）10－68326333
电子信箱：sinolingua@ihw.com.cn
北京外文印刷厂印刷
中国国际图书贸易总公司发行
（中国北京车公庄西路 35 号）
北京邮政信箱第 399 号　邮政编码 100044
新华书店国内发行
2002 年（34 开）第一版
（汉英）
ISBN 7－80052－806－5/H·1262（外）
9－CE－3478P
定价：22.00 元